Stinky Clothes

Written by Joanna Emery
Illustrated by Richard Rossi

Children's Press®
A Division of Scholastic Inc.
New York • Toronto • London • Auckland • Sydney
Mexico City • New Delhi • Hong Kong
Danbury, Connecticut

For my children, Veronica, Monty, and Mimi.
—J.E.

Thanks, Pop.
—R.R.

Consultant

Eileen Robinson
Reading Specialist

Library of Congress Cataloging-in-Publication Data
Emery, Joanna.
 Stinky clothes / written by Joanna Emery ; illustrated by Richard Rossi.
  p. cm. — (A rookie reader)
 Summary: A rhyming story about a child doing the laundry.
 ISBN 0-516-25151-1 (lib. bdg.)   0-516-25284-4 (pbk.)

 [1. Laundry—Fiction. 2. Stories in rhyme.] I. Rossi, Richard, 1960- ill. II. Title. III.
Series.

 PZ8.3.E523St 2004
 [E]—dc22

                    2004009330

CHILDREN'S PRESS, and A ROOKIE READER®, and associated logos are
trademarks and or registered trademarks of Scholastic Library Publishing.
SCHOLASTIC and associated logos are trademarks and or registered trademarks of
Scholastic Inc.
1 2 3 4 5 6 7 8 9 10 R 14 13 12 11 10 09 08 07 06 05

Hold your nose around stinky clothes!

The washing machine will get them clean.

The clothes go in.

Hear that spin?

8

When it's done,
out they come.

They feel heavy.

They feel wet.

The laundry is not finished yet.

I hang them up one by one.
I let them dry under the sun.

17

18

Hear that plop?
Feel that drop?

Here comes rain!
I take them down again.

The dryer makes a rumble sound.
The clothes inside tumble around.

I match the socks.

24

I do them first.

I roll the towels,
then hang the shirts.

I put all my other clothes away.

No more stinky clothes today!

Word List (72 Words)

a	first	more	sun
again	get	my	take
all	go	no	that
around	hang	nose	the
away	hear	not	them
by	heavy	one	then
clean	here	other	they
clothes	hold	out	today
come	I	plop	towels
comes	in	put	tumble
do	inside	rain	under
done	is	roll	up
down	it's	rumble	washing
drop	laundry	shirts	wet
dry	let	socks	when
dryer	machine	sound	will
feel	makes	spin	yet
finished	match	stinky	your

About the Author

Joanna Emery has been writing for children of all ages for over a decade. One of her favorite memories was the time she made an author visit to a school in Tarsus, Turkey. She lives in Ontario, Canada, with her husband, Greg, their three children and four cats. She always has lots of laundry to do.

About the Illustrator

Richard Rossi is a New Jersey based freelance illustrator. He has worked on numerous children's books, greeting cards, and editorial works. He graduated from Syracuse University, and is married with two children.